This Journal belongs to

_____

_____

Mood tracker

January

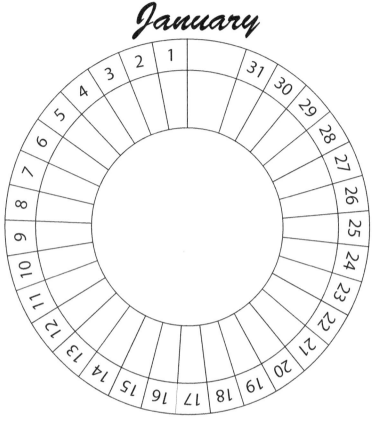

February

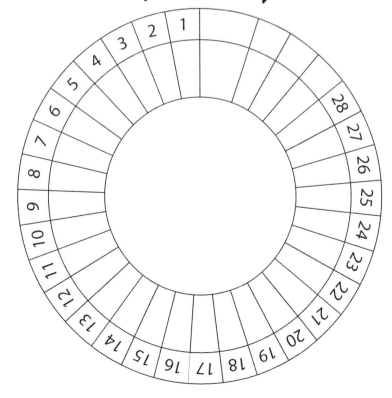

Angry	
Annoyed	
Anxious	
Ashamed	
Confused	
Energetic	
Excited	
Exsausted	
Happy	
Sad	

Mood tracker

March

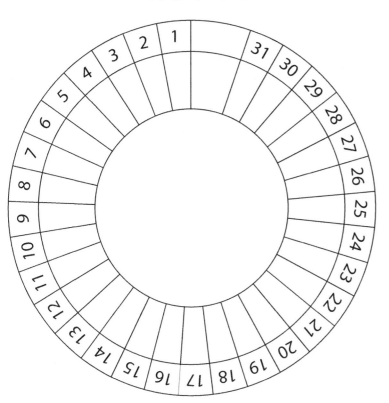

April

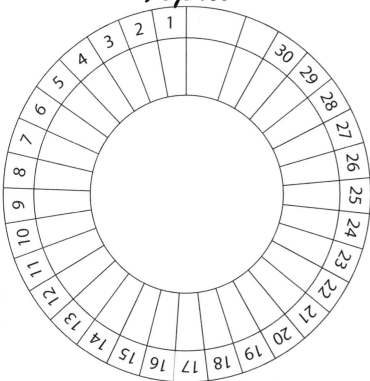

Angry	
Annoyed	
Anxious	
Ashamed	
Confused	
Energetic	
Excited	
Exsausted	
Happy	
Sad	

Mood tracker

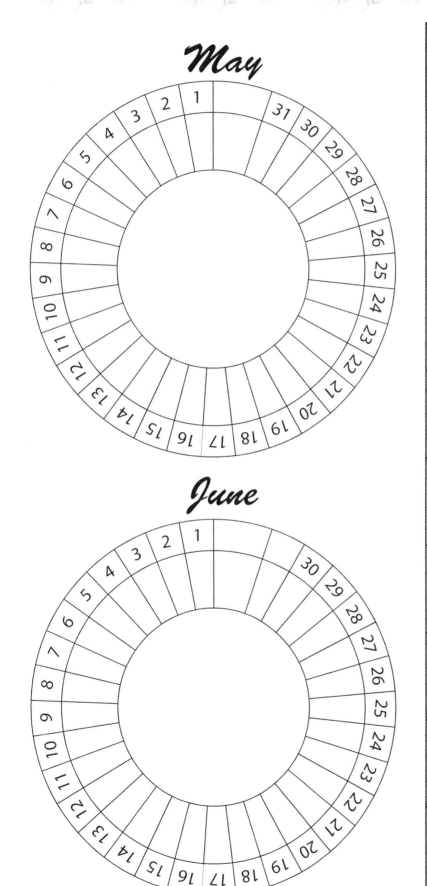

May

June

Angry	
Annoyed	
Anxious	
Ashamed	
Confused	
Energetic	
Excited	
Exsausted	
Happy	
Sad	

Mood tracker

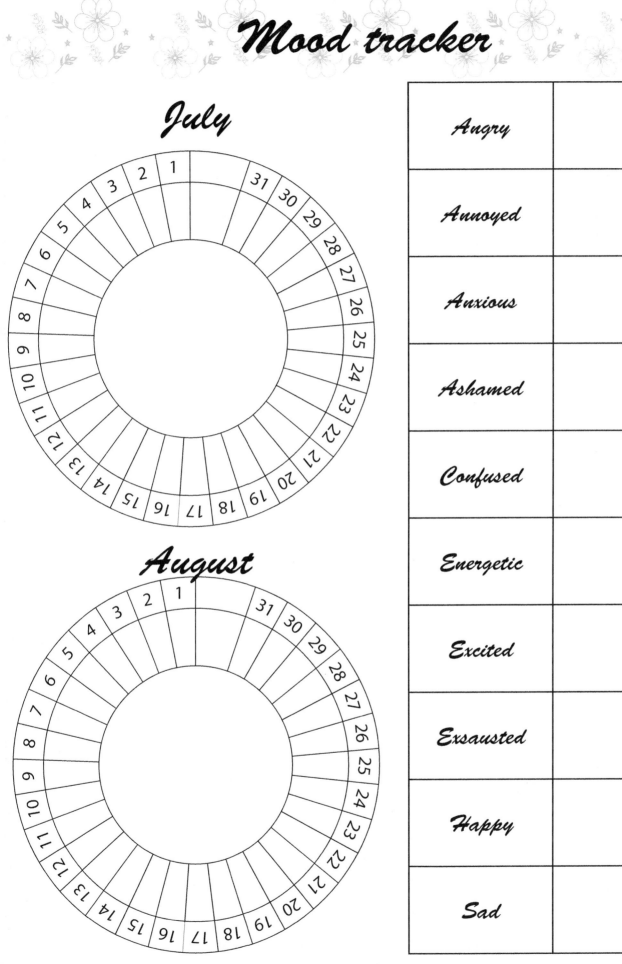

July

August

Angry	
Annoyed	
Anxious	
Ashamed	
Confused	
Energetic	
Excited	
Exsausted	
Happy	
Sad	

Mood tracker

September

October

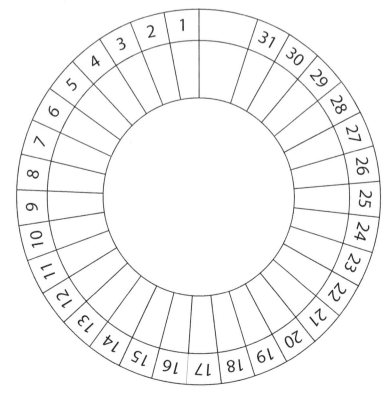

Angry	
Annoyed	
Anxious	
Ashamed	
Confused	
Energetic	
Excited	
Exsausted	
Happy	
Sad	

Mood tracker

November

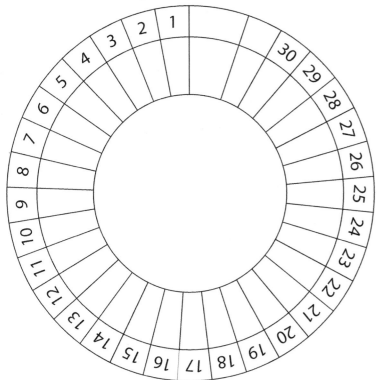

December

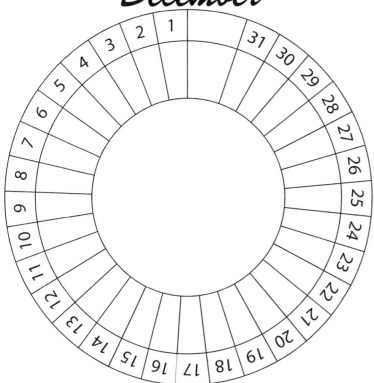

Angry	
Annoyed	
Anxious	
Ashamed	
Confused	
Energetic	
Excited	
Exsausted	
Happy	
Sad	

My day

Date:

How do I feel?

Today's thoughts

Today I am grateful for

Something I did well today

_____

_____

I had fun when

_____

_____

I felt proud when

_____

_____

Things that made me smile

_____

_____

I will accomplish these 3 goals:

1 _____

2 _____

3 _____

My day

Date:

How do I feel?

Today's thoughts

Today I am grateful for

Something I did well today

_____

_____

I had fun when

_____

_____

I felt proud when

_____

_____

Things that made me smile

_____

_____

I will accomplish these 3 goals:

1 _____

2 _____

3 _____

My day

Date:

How do I feel?

Today's thoughts

Today I am grateful for

Something I did well today

_____

_____

I had fun when

_____

_____

I felt proud when

_____

_____

Things that made me smile

_____

_____

I will accomplish these 3 goals:

1 _____

2 _____

3 _____

My day

Date:

How do I feel?

Today's thoughts

Today I am grateful for

Something I did well today

_____

_____

I had fun when

_____

_____

I felt proud when

_____

_____

Things that made me smile

_____

_____

I will accomplish these 3 goals:

1 _____

2 _____

3 _____

My day

Date:

How do I feel?

Today's thoughts

Today I am grateful for

Something I did well today

_____

_____

I had fun when

_____

_____

I felt proud when

_____

_____

Things that made me smile

_____

_____

I will accomplish these 3 goals:

1 _____

2 _____

3 _____

My day

Date:

How do I feel?

Today's thoughts

Today I am grateful for

Something I did well today

_____

_____

I had fun when

_____

_____

I felt proud when

_____

_____

Things that made me smile

_____

_____

I will accomplish these 3 goals:

1 _____

2 _____

3 _____

My day

Date:

How do I feel?

Today's thoughts

Today I am grateful for

Something I did well today

_____

_____

I had fun when

_____

_____

I felt proud when

_____

_____

Things that made me smile

_____

_____

I will accomplish these 3 goals:

1 _____

2 _____

3 _____

My day

Date:

How do I feel?

Today's thoughts

Today I am grateful for

Something I did well today

_____

_____

I had fun when

_____

_____

I felt proud when

_____

_____

Things that made me smile

_____

_____

I will accomplish these 3 goals:

1 _____

2 _____

3 _____

My day

Date:

How do I feel?

Today's thoughts

Today I am grateful for

Something I did well today

_____

_____

I had fun when

_____

_____

I felt proud when

_____

_____

Things that made me smile

_____

_____

I will accomplish these 3 goals:

1 _____

2 _____

3 _____

My day

Date:

How do I feel?

Today's thoughts

Today I am grateful for

Something I did well today

_____

_____

I had fun when

_____

_____

I felt proud when

_____

_____

Things that made me smile

_____

_____

I will accomplish these 3 goals:

1 _____

2 _____

3 _____

My day

Date:

How do I feel?

Today's thoughts

Today I am grateful for

Something I did well today

_____

_____

I had fun when

_____

_____

I felt proud when

_____

_____

Things that made me smile

_____

_____

I will accomplish these 3 goals:

1 _____

2 _____

3 _____

My day

Date:

How do I feel?

Today's thoughts

Today I am grateful for

Something I did well today

_____

_____

I had fun when

_____

_____

I felt proud when

_____

_____

Things that made me smile

_____

_____

I will accomplish these 3 goals:

1 _____

2 _____

3 _____

My day

Date:

How do I feel?

Today's thoughts

Today I am grateful for

Something I did well today

_____

_____

I had fun when

_____

_____

I felt proud when

_____

_____

Things that made me smile

_____

_____

I will accomplish these 3 goals:

1 _____

2 _____

3 _____

My day

Date:

How do I feel?

Today's thoughts

Today I am grateful for

Something I did well today

_____

_____

I had fun when

_____

_____

I felt proud when

_____

_____

Things that made me smile

_____

_____

I will accomplish these 3 goals:

1 _____

2 _____

3 _____

My day

Date:

How do I feel?

Today's thoughts

Today I am grateful for

Something I did well today

_____

_____

I had fun when

_____

_____

I felt proud when

_____

_____

Things that made me smile

_____

_____

I will accomplish these 3 goals:

1 _____

2 _____

3 _____

My day

Date:

How do I feel?

Today's thoughts

Today I am grateful for

Something I did well today

_____

_____

I had fun when

_____

_____

I felt proud when

_____

_____

Things that made me smile

_____

_____

I will accomplish these 3 goals:

1 _____

2 _____

3 _____

My day

Date:

How do I feel?

Today's thoughts

Today I am grateful for

Something I did well today

_____

_____

I had fun when

_____

_____

I felt proud when

_____

_____

Things that made me smile

_____

_____

I will accomplish these 3 goals:

1 _____

2 _____

3 _____

My day

Date:

How do I feel?

Today's thoughts

Today I am grateful for

Something I did well today

_____

_____

I had fun when

_____

_____

I felt proud when

_____

_____

Things that made me smile

_____

_____

I will accomplish these 3 goals:

1 _____

2 _____

3 _____

My day

Date:

How do I feel?

Today's thoughts

Today I am grateful for

Something I did well today

_____

_____

I had fun when

_____

_____

I felt proud when

_____

_____

Things that made me smile

_____

_____

I will accomplish these 3 goals:

1 _____

2 _____

3 _____

My day

Date:

How do I feel?

Today's thoughts

Today I am grateful for

Something I did well today

_____

_____

I had fun when

_____

_____

I felt proud when

_____

_____

Things that made me smile

_____

_____

I will accomplish these 3 goals:

1 _____

2 _____

3 _____

My day

Date:

How do I feel?

Today's thoughts

Today I am grateful for

Something I did well today

_____

_____

I had fun when

_____

_____

I felt proud when

_____

_____

Things that made me smile

_____

_____

I will accomplish these 3 goals:

1 _____

2 _____

3 _____

My day

Date:

How do I feel?

Today's thoughts

Today I am grateful for

Something I did well today

_____

_____

I had fun when

_____

_____

I felt proud when

_____

_____

Things that made me smile

_____

_____

I will accomplish these 3 goals:

1 _____

2 _____

3 _____

My day

Date:

How do I feel?

Today's thoughts

Today I am grateful for

Something I did well today

_____

_____

I had fun when

_____

_____

I felt proud when

_____

_____

Things that made me smile

_____

_____

I will accomplish these 3 goals:

1 _____

2 _____

3 _____

My day

Date:

How do I feel?

Today's thoughts

Today I am grateful for

Something I did well today

_____

_____

I had fun when

_____

_____

I felt proud when

_____

_____

Things that made me smile

_____

_____

I will accomplish these 3 goals:

1 _____

2 _____

3 _____

My day

Date:

How do I feel?

Today's thoughts

Today I am grateful for

Something I did well today

_____

_____

I had fun when

_____

_____

I felt proud when

_____

_____

Things that made me smile

_____

_____

I will accomplish these 3 goals:

1 _____

2 _____

3 _____

My day

Date:

How do I feel?

Today's thoughts

Today I am grateful for

Something I did well today

_____

_____

I had fun when

_____

_____

I felt proud when

_____

_____

Things that made me smile

_____

_____

I will accomplish these 3 goals:

1 _____

2 _____

3 _____

My day

Date:

How do I feel?

Today's thoughts

Today I am grateful for

Something I did well today

_____

_____

I had fun when

_____

_____

I felt proud when

_____

_____

Things that made me smile

_____

_____

I will accomplish these 3 goals:

1 _____

2 _____

3 _____

My day

Date:

How do I feel?

Today's thoughts

Today I am grateful for

Something I did well today

_____

_____

I had fun when

_____

_____

I felt proud when

_____

_____

Things that made me smile

_____

_____

I will accomplish these 3 goals:

1 _____

2 _____

3 _____

My day

Date:

How do I feel?

Today's thoughts

Today I am grateful for

Something I did well today

_____

_____

I had fun when

_____

_____

I felt proud when

_____

_____

Things that made me smile

_____

_____

I will accomplish these 3 goals:

1 _____

2 _____

3 _____

My day

Date:

How do I feel?

Today's thoughts

Today I am grateful for

Something I did well today

_____

_____

I had fun when

_____

_____

I felt proud when

_____

_____

Things that made me smile

_____

_____

I will accomplish these 3 goals:

1 _____

2 _____

3 _____

My day

Date:

How do I feel?

Today's thoughts

Today I am grateful for

Something I did well today

_____

_____

I had fun when

_____

_____

I felt proud when

_____

_____

Things that made me smile

_____

_____

I will accomplish these 3 goals:

1 _____

2 _____

3 _____

My day

Date:

How do I feel?

Today's thoughts

Today I am grateful for

Something I did well today

_____

_____

I had fun when

_____

_____

I felt proud when

_____

_____

Things that made me smile

_____

_____

I will accomplish these 3 goals:

1 _____

2 _____

3 _____

My day

Date:

How do I feel?

Today's thoughts

Today I am grateful for

Something I did well today

_____

_____

I had fun when

_____

_____

I felt proud when

_____

_____

Things that made me smile

_____

_____

I will accomplish these 3 goals:

1 _____

2 _____

3 _____

My day

Date:

How do I feel?

Today's thoughts

Today I am grateful for

Something I did well today

_____

_____

I had fun when

_____

_____

I felt proud when

_____

_____

Things that made me smile

_____

_____

I will accomplish these 3 goals:

1 _____

2 _____

3 _____

My day

Date:

How do I feel?

Today's thoughts

Today I am grateful for

Something I did well today

_____

_____

I had fun when

_____

_____

I felt proud when

_____

_____

Things that made me smile

_____

_____

I will accomplish these 3 goals:

1 _____

2 _____

3 _____

My day

Date:

How do I feel?

Today's thoughts

Today I am grateful for

Something I did well today

_____

_____

I had fun when

_____

_____

I felt proud when

_____

_____

Things that made me smile

_____

_____

I will accomplish these 3 goals:

1 _____

2 _____

3 _____

My day

Date:

How do I feel?

Today's thoughts

Today I am grateful for

Something I did well today

_____

_____

I had fun when

_____

_____

I felt proud when

_____

_____

Things that made me smile

_____

_____

I will accomplish these 3 goals:

1 _____

2 _____

3 _____

My day

Date:

How do I feel?

Today's thoughts

Today I am grateful for

Something I did well today

_____

_____

I had fun when

_____

_____

I felt proud when

_____

_____

Things that made me smile

_____

_____

I will accomplish these 3 goals:

1 _____

2 _____

3 _____

My day

Date:

How do I feel?

Today's thoughts

Today I am grateful for

Something I did well today

_____

_____

I had fun when

_____

_____

I felt proud when

_____

_____

Things that made me smile

_____

_____

I will accomplish these 3 goals:

1 _____

2 _____

3 _____

My day

Date:

How do I feel?

Today's thoughts

Today I am grateful for

Something I did well today

_____

_____

I had fun when

_____

_____

I felt proud when

_____

_____

Things that made me smile

_____

_____

I will accomplish these 3 goals:

1 _____

2 _____

3 _____

My day

Date:

How do I feel?

Today's thoughts

Today I am grateful for

Something I did well today

_____

_____

I had fun when

_____

_____

I felt proud when

_____

_____

Things that made me smile

_____

_____

I will accomplish these 3 goals:

1 _____

2 _____

3 _____

My day

Date:

How do I feel?

Today's thoughts

Today I am grateful for

Something I did well today

_____

_____

I had fun when

_____

_____

I felt proud when

_____

_____

Things that made me smile

_____

_____

I will accomplish these 3 goals:

1 _____

2 _____

3 _____

My day

Date:

How do I feel?

Today's thoughts

Today I am grateful for

Something I did well today

_____

_____

I had fun when

_____

_____

I felt proud when

_____

_____

Things that made me smile

_____

_____

I will accomplish these 3 goals:

1 _____

2 _____

3 _____

My day

Date:

How do I feel?

Today's thoughts

Today I am grateful for

Something I did well today

_____

_____

I had fun when

_____

_____

I felt proud when

_____

_____

Things that made me smile

_____

_____

I will accomplish these 3 goals:

1 _____

2 _____

3 _____

My day

Date:

How do I feel?

Today's thoughts

Today I am grateful for

Something I did well today

_____

_____

I had fun when

_____

_____

I felt proud when

_____

_____

Things that made me smile

_____

_____

I will accomplish these 3 goals:

1 _____

2 _____

3 _____

My day

Date:

How do I feel?

Today's thoughts

Today I am grateful for

Something I did well today

_____

_____

I had fun when

_____

_____

I felt proud when

_____

_____

Things that made me smile

_____

_____

I will accomplish these 3 goals:

1 _____

2 _____

3 _____

My day

Date:

How do I feel?

Today's thoughts

Today I am grateful for

Something I did well today

_____

_____

I had fun when

_____

_____

I felt proud when

_____

_____

Things that made me smile

_____

_____

I will accomplish these 3 goals:

1 _____

2 _____

3 _____

Printed in Great Britain
by Amazon